Confident Girls!

Confidence & Purpose Building Activities for Girls

By

Bridget Moore

Bridget Moore
www.buildingconfidentgirls.com

ISBN 978-1-941749-33-3

Limits of Liability and Disclaimer of Warranty

The author and publisher shall not be liable for your misuse of this material. This book is strictly for informational and educational purposes.

Warning – Disclaimer

The purpose of this book is to educate and entertain. The author and/or publisher do not guarantee that anyone following these techniques, suggestions, tips, ideas, or strategies will become successful. The author and/or publisher shall have neither liability nor responsibility to anyone with respect to any loss or damage caused, or alleged to be caused, directly or indirectly by the information contained in this book.

Certain definitions provided by Encarta, merriam-webster.com and dictionary.com.

Image(s) or Footage (as applicable), used under license from Shutterstock.com

Illustration (Cover, life path, seed progression, and girls playing board game) by Kamui Ayami

Editing by Sylvia Banks

4-P Publishing

Chattanooga, TN 37411

Dedication

Thanks to all the helping hands, encouraging words and support from my family and friends. A special thanks to my loving and supportive husband, Geoffrey and our beautiful children Brianna, Geoffrey Jr. and Gabriel.

May this book empower girls to grow into confident, purpose filled women!

PURPOSE

Have you ever wondered why people are born? Well, we are here for a reason! We all have a gift that can make others happy or help them in some way. There may be things that are easy for you to do, but may be difficult for someone else. You can have an effect on others by giving, helping, sharing and caring! With the help from everyone, we all can change the world!

Purpose For Everything

Everything that I see

has a purpose, even me!

The sun, water, land, and trees

Are here to help us to live, you see.

Up above in the sky so bright,

Are the moon and stars we see each night.

The earth is full of all types of life,

We should always try to do what's right!

The ABC's Of You!
The words below describe some of the many qualities that you have!

Adorable- very appealing or attractive; very lovable

Beautiful- possessing qualities that give great pleasure

Charming- having the power to delight

Divine- unusually lovely

Elegant- stylish and graceful

Fantastic- extraordinarily good

Gorgeous-very enjoyable or pleasant

Honest- good and truthful

Imaginative- skilled at visualizing or thinking originally

Joy- feelings of great happiness

Kind- showing compassion

Lovely- very pleasing, graceful

Marvelous- excellent or great

Nice- polite, kind or friendly

Original- a unique person who is different

Powerful- qualities that produce a fast and effective result

Quality- the highest or finest standard

Remarkable- worthy of notice or attention

Superb- the highest quality

Terrific- extremely good; wonderful

Unique- one of a kind

Value- wealth or importance

Worthy- good and deserving respect, praise, or attention

Youthful- having the freshness or energy of someone who is young

Zest-exciting and enjoyable quality

Find the words

Purpose –
Reason for existence

```
X Z K V H P B P H T P A
O I J F E D L T H N O J
C I A N U W R A O E S U
A S S I G N M E N T I L
P R C D I I C P H N T R
O Q J L Q A S T F I I A
F G D M L N P E I F O F
J R A L O U E Z D O N C
N O I S S I M W B H N V
C N A I D E A L D I N L
G E K X Y C B K G A H E
R D H T U D S I R U B U
```

ASSIGNMENT
CALLING
DESIGN
FUNCTION
IDEA

INTENT
MISSION
PLAN
POSITION
REASON

"Be what you WANT to be

NOT what OTHERS want to SEE"

Match the letters with each number to decode an important message!

26	64	28		6	93	25	93

9	2	4	93	64	35

13	28	25	13	64	17	93

54	64	25	2

13	28	25	13	64	17	93

2	72	11	4
A	B	C	D

93	54	37	81
E	F	G	H

7	33	44	91
I	J	K	L

9	35	64	13
M	N	0	P

53	25	17	19
Q	R	S	T

28	51	6	5
U	V	W	X

26	0
Y	Z

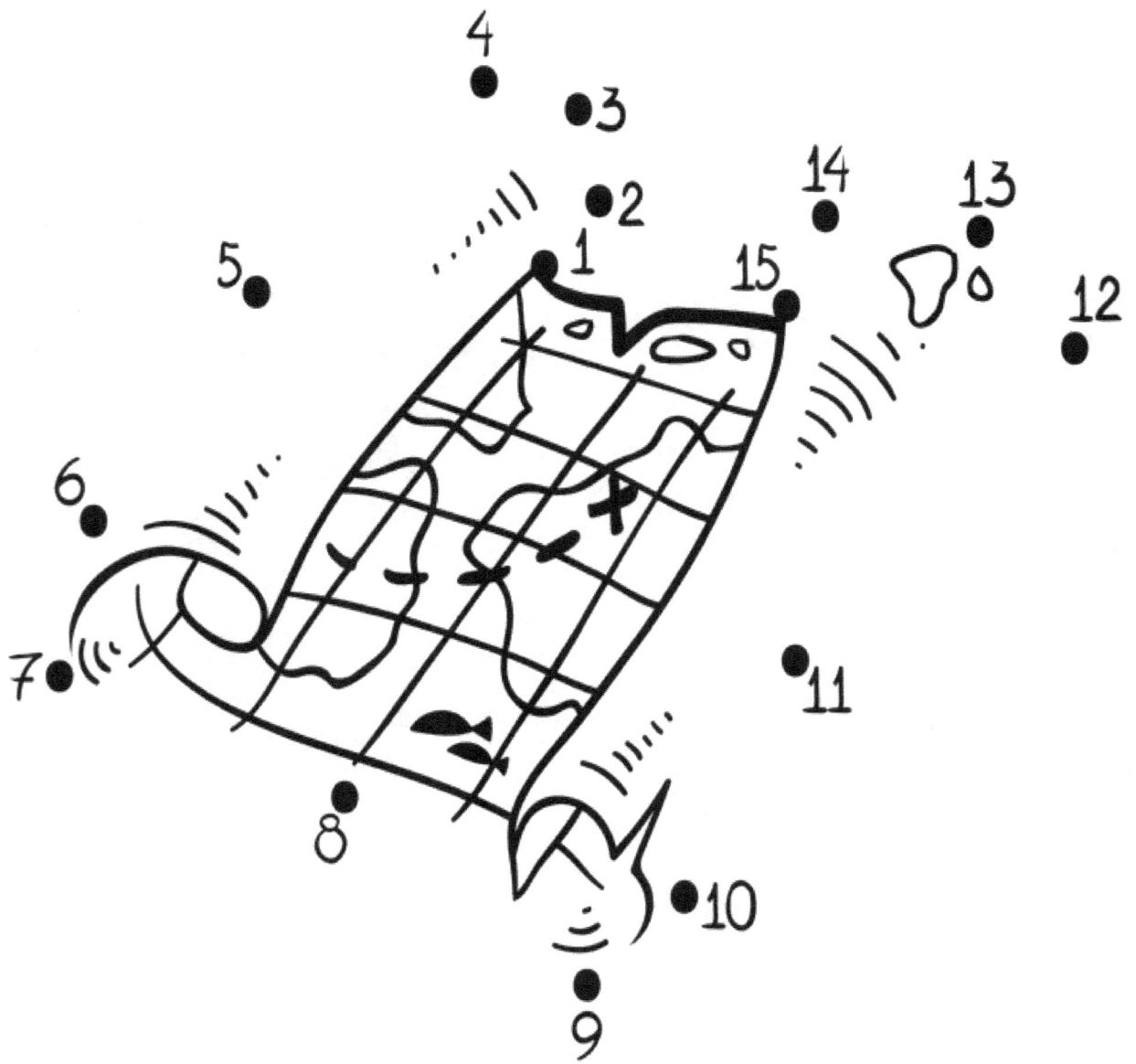

Your treasure lies with your purpose!

Match the color with the number to complete the picture!

1 - White	5 - Tan
2 - Blue	6 - Orange
3 - Light Green	7 - Brown
4 - Dark Green	8 - Gray

YOU WILL NEVER KNOW UNTIL YOU TRY

Within you IS THE STRENGTH to FULFILL all your dreams.

Declarations

A declaration is statement that is true or
something that you want to see happen.
Read the sentences below every day
until you believe them!

I am *ACCEPTED*

I am *BEAUTIFUL*

I am *BRAVE*

I am *SMART*

I am *FUNNY*

I am *FRIENDLY*

I am *GIVING*

I am *GOOD*

I am *HAPPY*

I am *KIND*

I am *UNIQUE*

I am *WONDERFUL*

I am *CALM*

I am *CONFIDENT*

I am *GIFTED*

I am *TALENTED*

I am *POLITE*

I am *WISE*

I am *PRECIOUS*

Declarations

What are some things you would like to
see yourself doing?
Where is a special place you would
like to go?
Write down your own declarations below
and read them daily!

_____

_____

_____

_____

_____

Follow Your Dreams!

Everyone has their own path in life.
Find yours and enjoy the journey!

Complete the picture, then color.

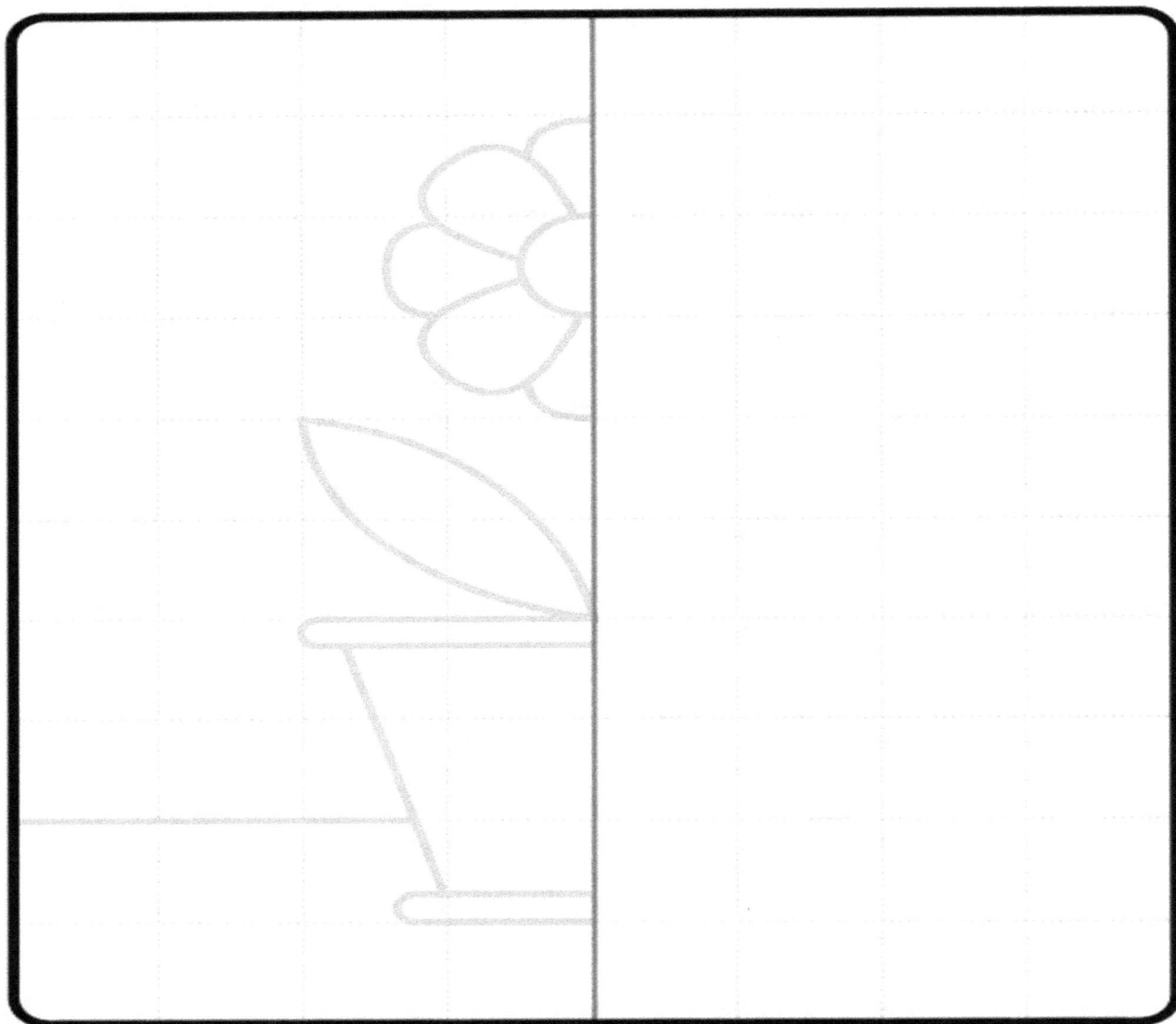

Today, have THE COURAGE to be the person YOU REALLY ARE.

ENJOY THE LITTLE THINGS

YOU ARE

A-MAZE-ING

You are a Leader!

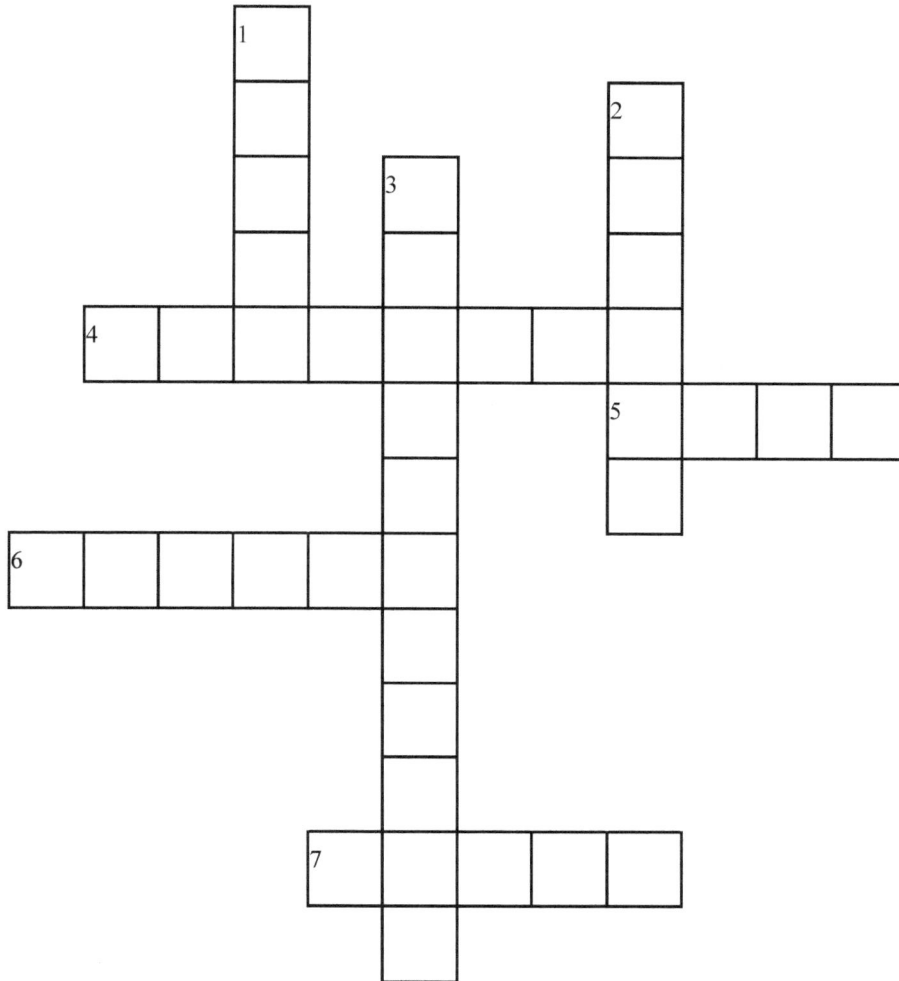

Across

4. Ready in advance

5. Ready and willing to accept or listen to new ideas or suggestions

6. A picture that you see in your mind; what can become

7. To concentrate on one main point or interest

Down

1. Feeling or showing no fear; not afraid

2. The ability to make good decisions and judgments

3. The ability to think of new things

WORD BANK

Brave
Focus
Imagination
Open
Prepared
Vision
Wisdom

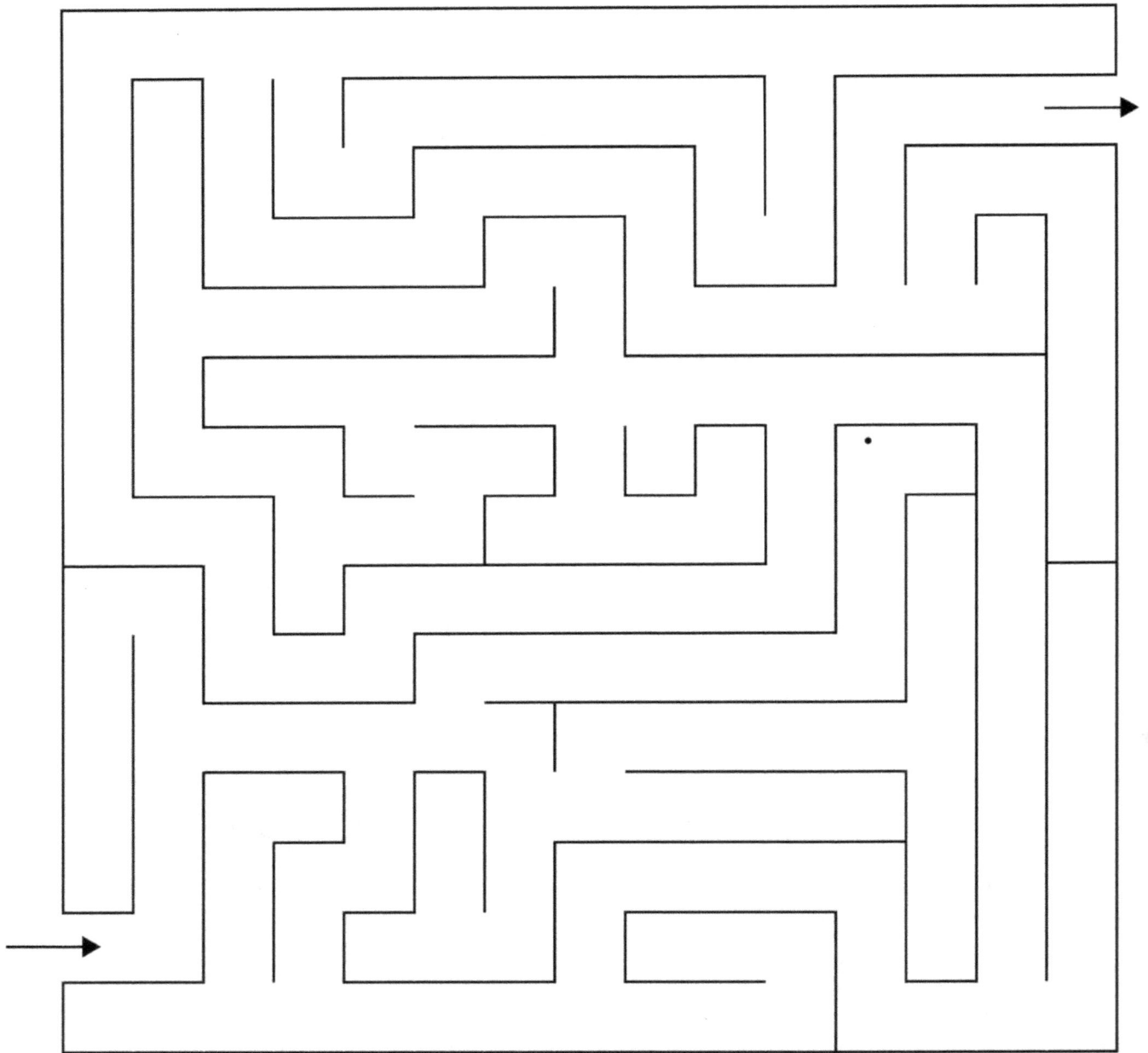

BELIEVE IN YOURSELF AND YOUR ABILITIES

1

2   3   4   5

15   7   6
16

14   8

13   9

12   11   10

Let your intuition (your inner voice) be your compass in life!

Find the path to the fruit trees!

Paint the life you want!

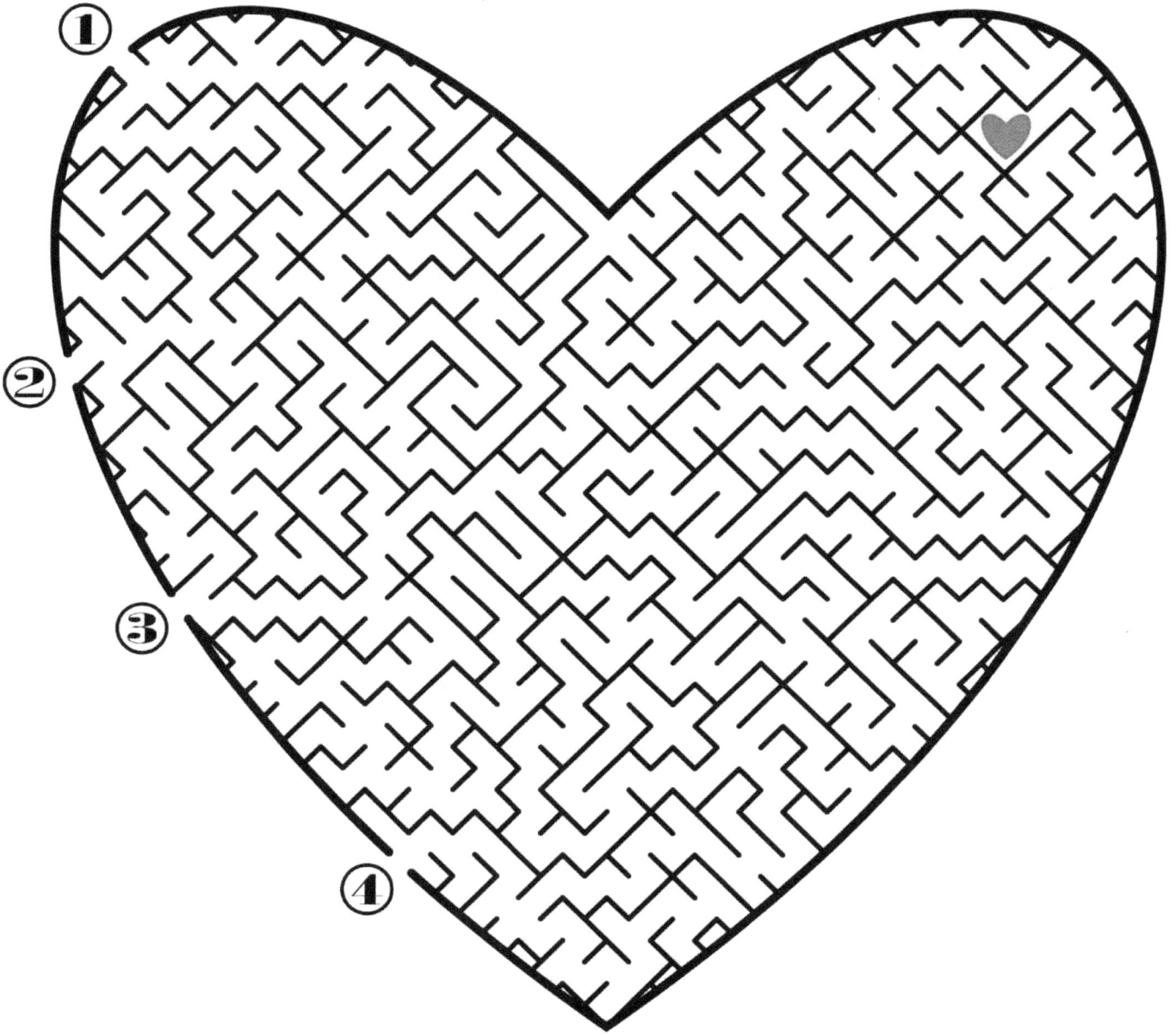

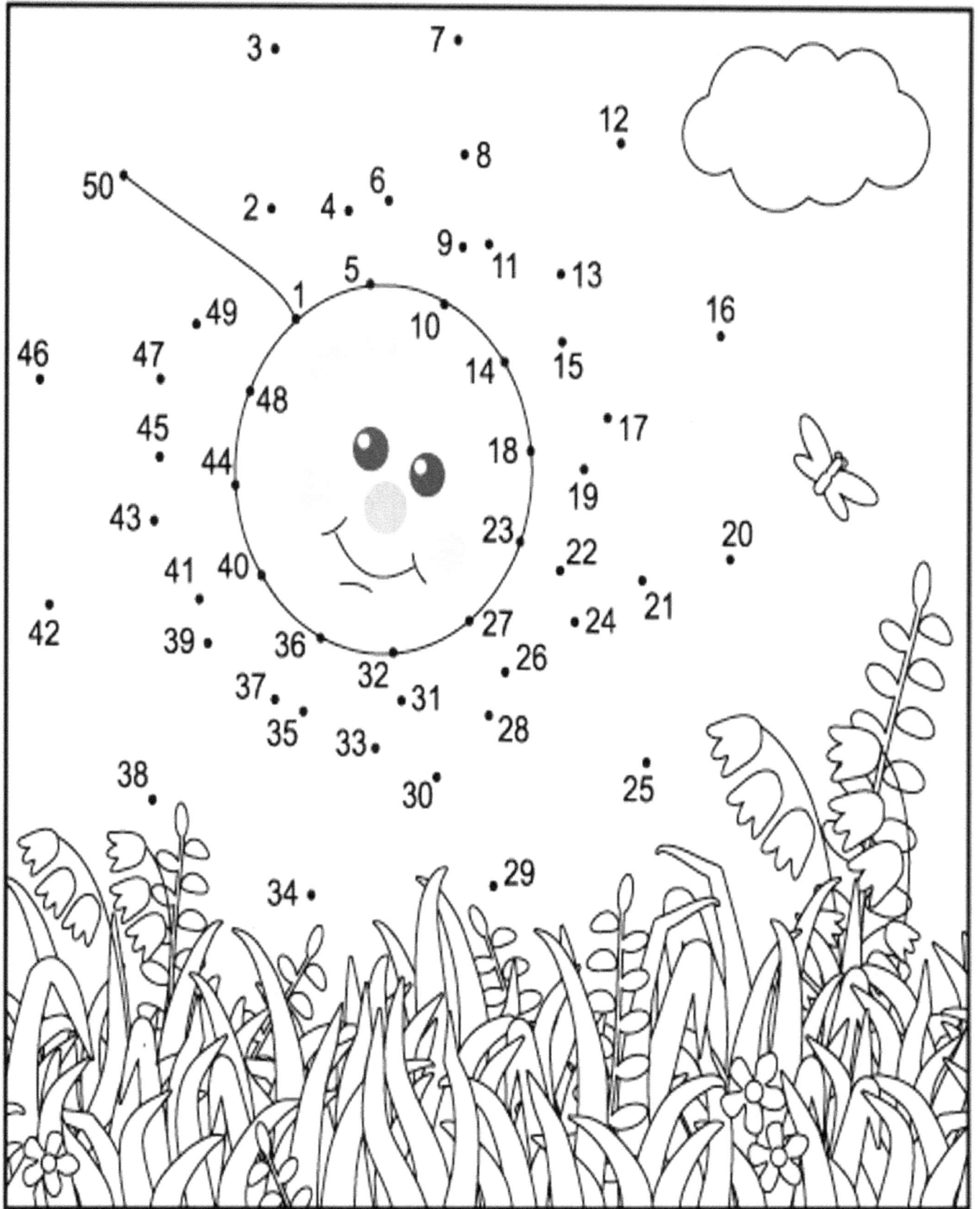

Find the words that describe all the wonderful things about you!

```
K D Z P U V J Y L T G L
C Q Y J R L O U J E I U
P D H G O E F Y L E V F
Q X L V A R C B H W I I
L V I Q E Y Q I U S N T
H N L D S X T W O B G U
G G N P O W E R F U L A
Q O E V A R B D A X S E
W Q U J Y A N H I M E B
H R P C P I Y N M B S Z
H T Z H K O M G K W C D
U R X F E B M N Q Q Y A
```

BEAUTIFUL

BRAVE

GIVING

KIND

LOVING

POWERFUL

PRECIOUS

SMART

SWEET

WONDERFUL

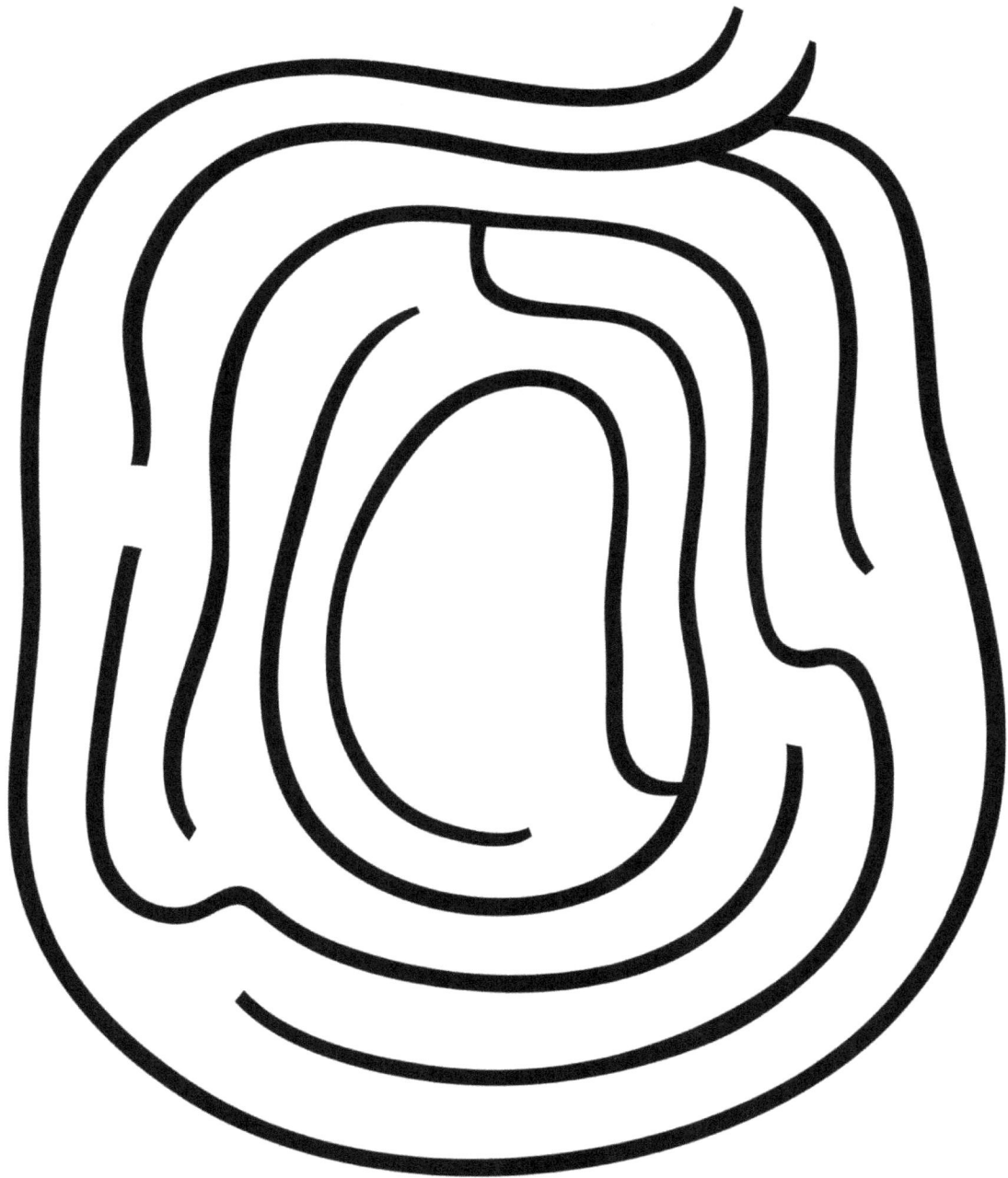

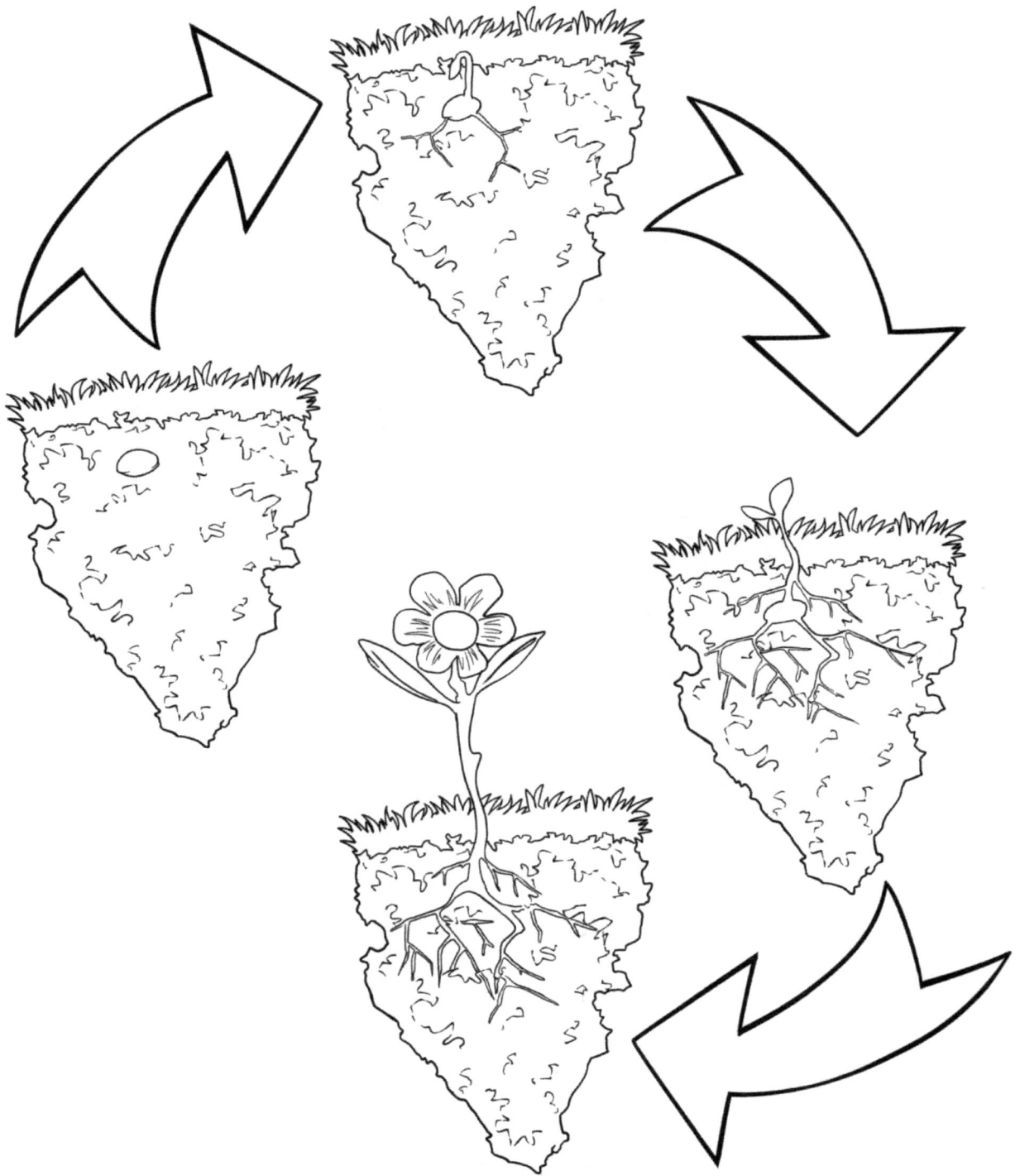

Like this plant, you will go

through different growth stages.

What does this plant need to be healthy and grow?
Circle the words below.

Water   Oil   Fire   Sun

          TV   Dirt   Nutrients

Time   Pizza   Air

Match the letters with each number to decode an important message!

17	81	2	25	93

26	64	28	25

37	7	54	19

6	7	19	81

19	81	93

6	64	25	91	4

2	72	11	4
A	B	C	D

93	54	37	81
E	F	G	H

7	33	44	91
I	J	K	L

9	35	64	13
M	N	0	P

53	25	17	19
Q	R	S	T

28	51	6	5
U	V	W	X

26	0
Y	Z

Complete the picture, then color.

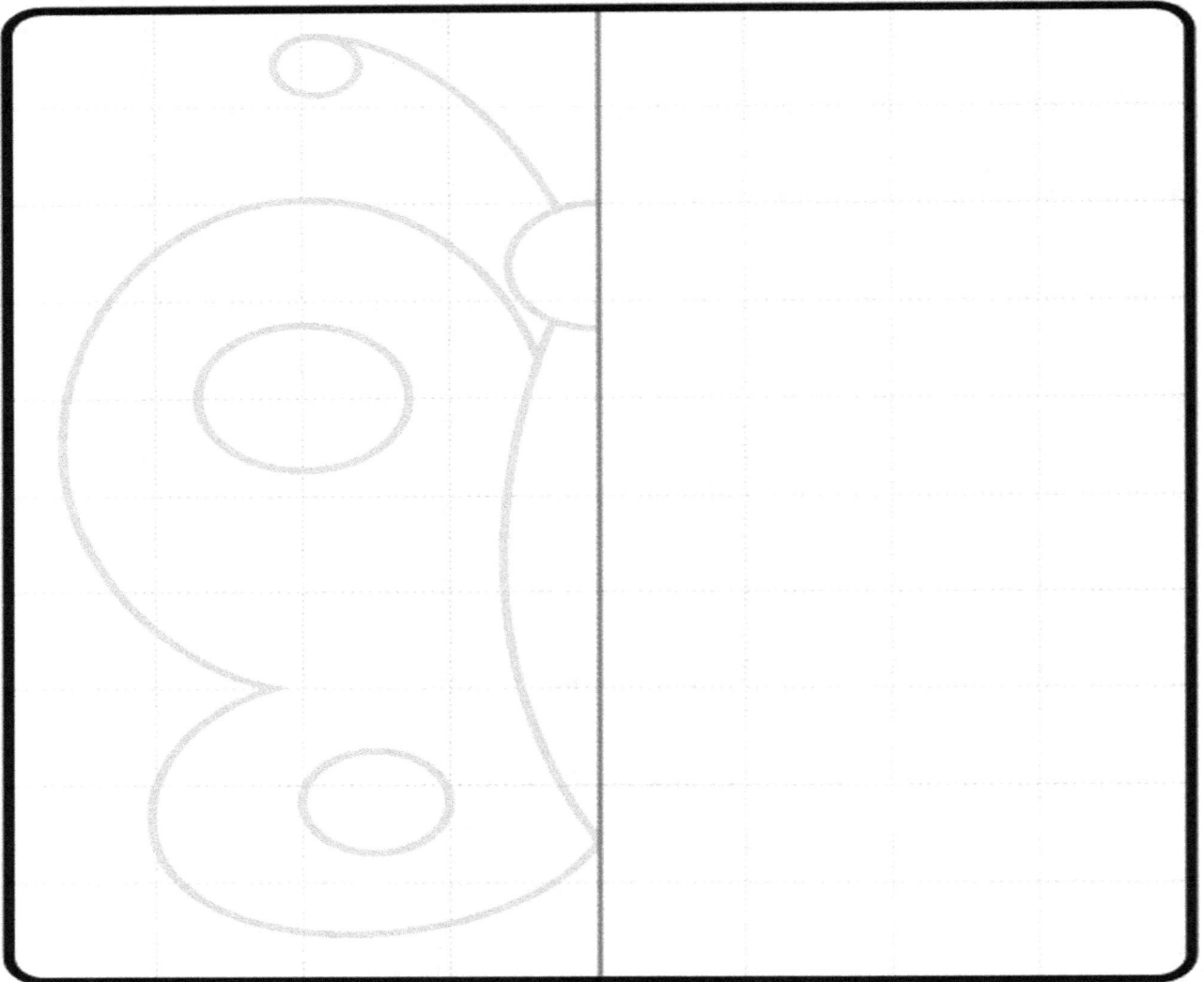

CONFIDENCE

Having confidence means that you are secure with who you are and your abilities. It doesn't matter what you wear or what you have, the only thing that matters lies within you. Do not change who you are just to fit in. Pick the right friends and always do what you feel is right. It is okay to make mistakes, just learn and don't repeat them. Set your mind on what you feel is right!

BECAUSE YOU'RE A GIRL!

Do you sometimes have doubts

Of what life is all about?

Don't worry, you are not alone.

We all have questions of where we belong.

You are beautiful, kind and smart

And you have a giving heart!

You're a courageous girl,

no you're not weak.

You have power, isn't that sweet?

You can do all things,

I know you may not be sure.

But you were given something special,

your gift is a cure.

Do what you love to change the world,

And you can do anything, because you're a girl!

Find the words!

Confidence-
Belief in your ability to succeed

```
K W T V Y R H E H O C S
A L B W O O F V G C J Q
O S T M Q S V I S E E R
B W S K G Q I S S R R N
K P O U G W E I P T U O
L S Z Z R L S C Q A S I
B K X A R E L E A I V E
O A Y A C V D D M N Y D
B J E U E V A R B R Y P
N F R P S I T Z I D I E
E E M Q E V V Y N M G F
V V P O S I T I V E Z V
```

ASSURED
BRAVE
CERTAIN
DECISIVE
FEARLESS
FIRM

POSITIVE
SECURE
SURE

Match the letters with each number to decode an important message!

72	93

19	25	28	93

19	64

26	64	28	25	17	93	91	54

2	72	11	4
A	B	C	D

93	54	37	81
E	F	G	H

7	33	44	91
I	J	K	L

9	35	64	13
M	N	0	P

53	25	17	19
Q	R	S	T

28	51	6	5
U	V	W	X

26	0
Y	Z

Unscramble the words below!

AREC _____

ONDF_____

ADLG_____

YJO_____

DINK_____

LEKI_____

VOEL_____

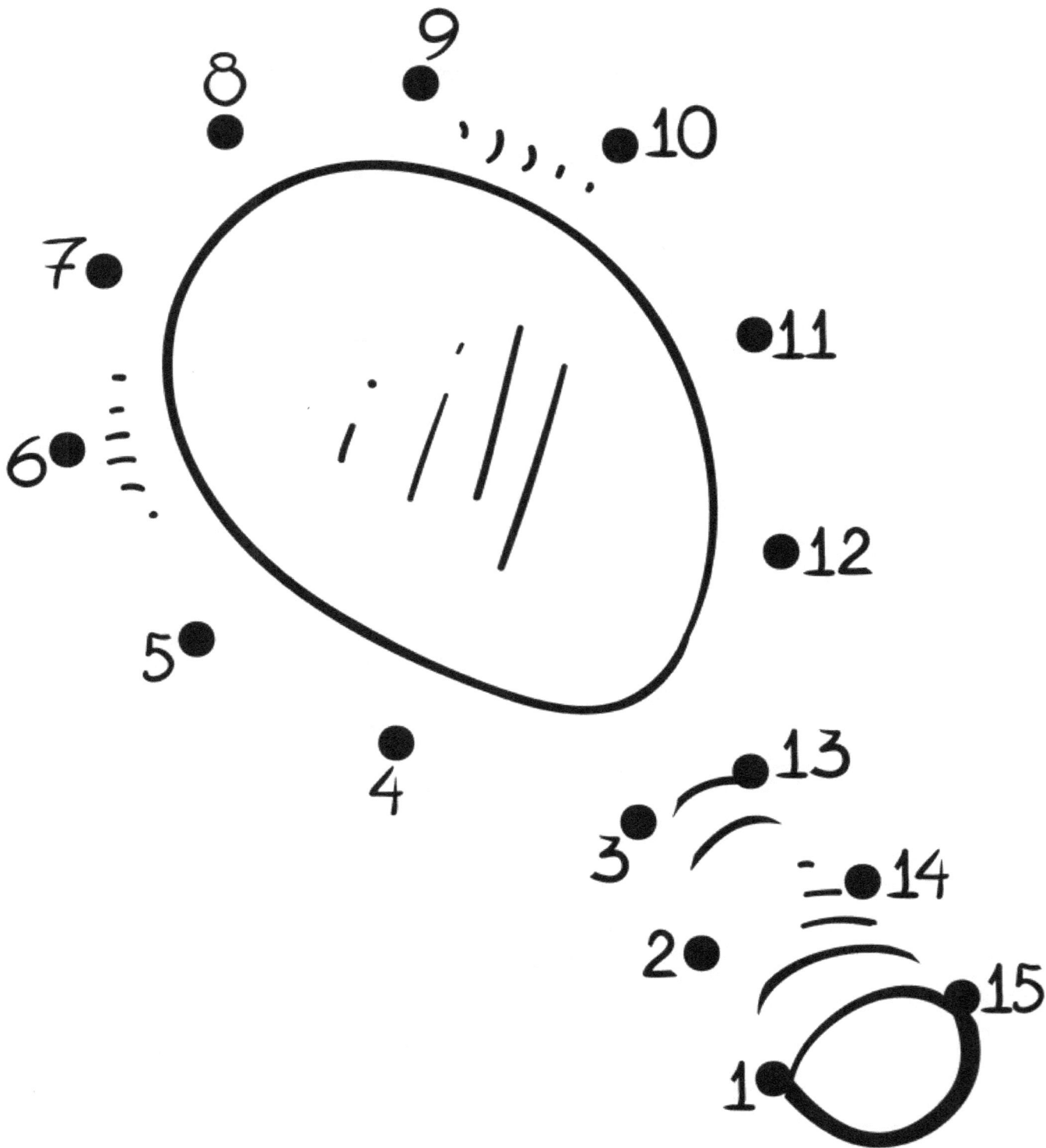

9

8

10

7

11

6

12

5

4

13

3

14

2

1

15

Circle the words that best describe being happy!

GLAD   CHEERFUL

FRIENDLY   HATE   SAD

HAPPY

JOY   ANGRY   MERRY

MAD   LOVING

Be happy with who you are!

Complete the picture, then color.

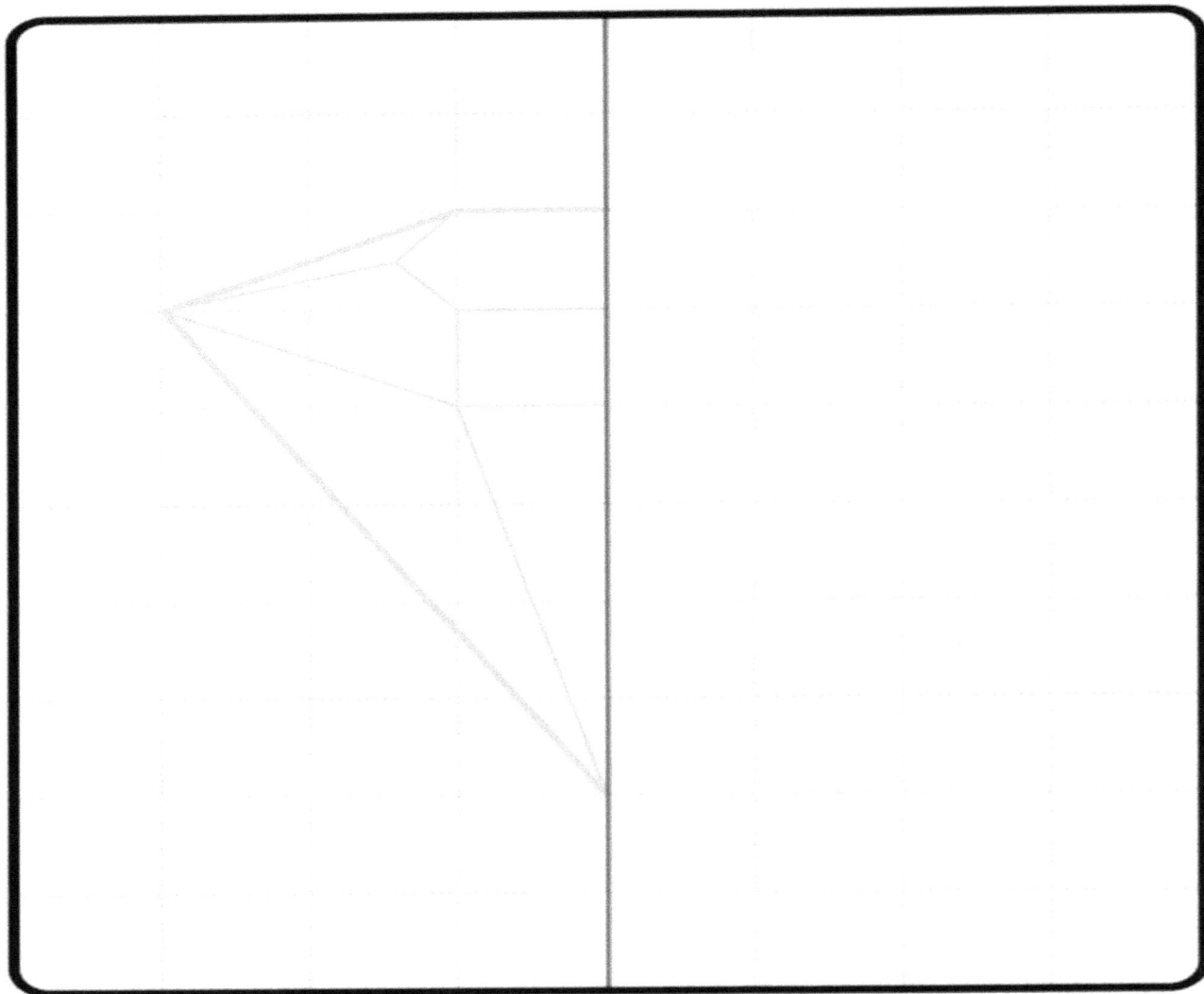

Choose friends that bring out the best in you!

HAPPINESS IS A CHOICE

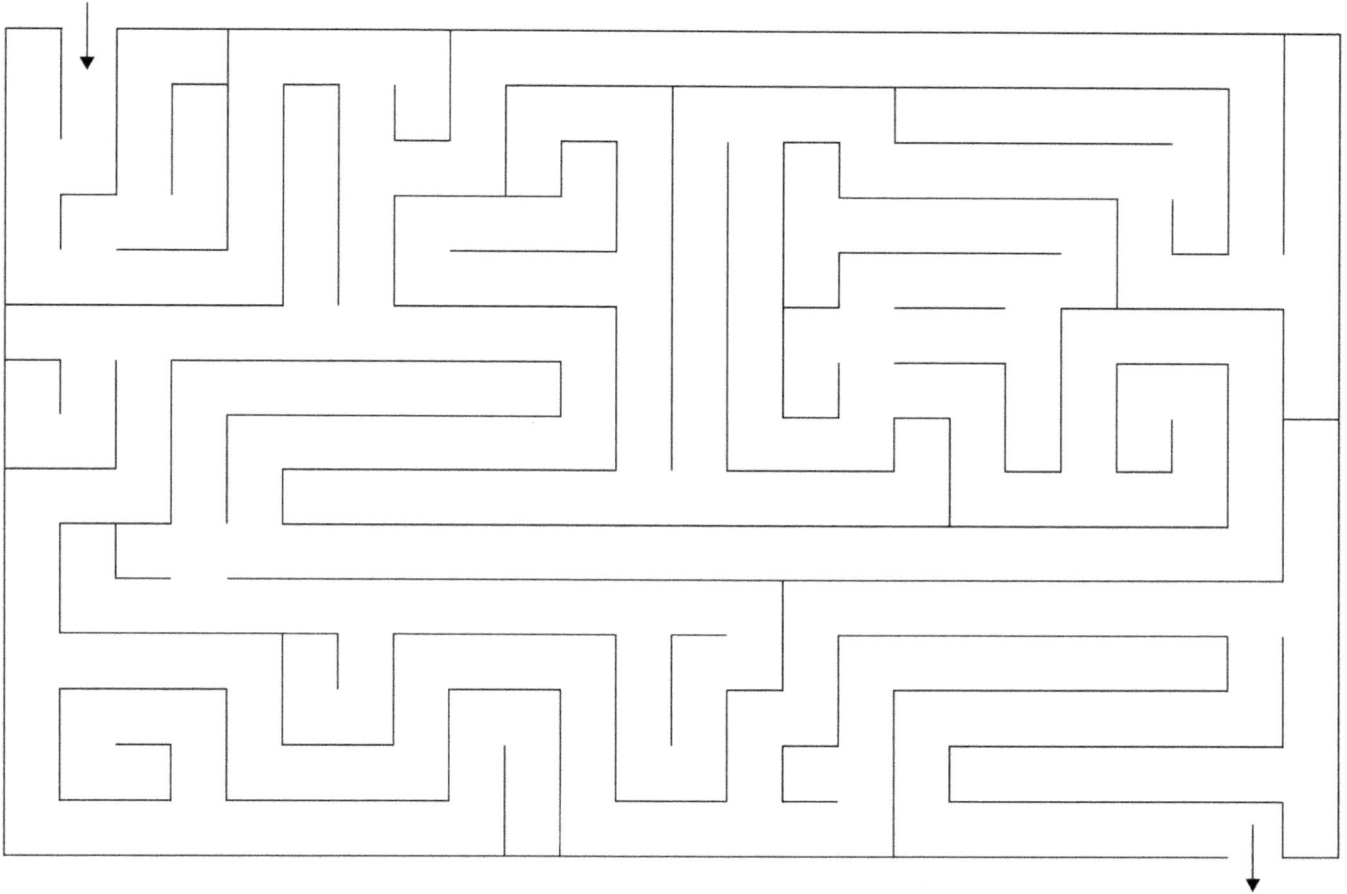

Don't Let Anyone Take Away Your Joy

Compliments

A compliment is something nice that you say.
Start the day by giving yourself a compliment,
then do the same for others throughout the day!

What are some things you like most about yourself?
What are some hobbies you are good at?
Write them down and work on them so you can
become the best YOU!

_____

_____

_____

_____

I AM STRONG, BRAVE AND NEVER AFRAID!

Use your imagination to draw your silliest face!

Have you ever heard of the phrase "Turn that frown upside down"?
Whenever you are sad, lonely or mad, try to remember a
time or place that made you happy!
Only you can determine your day!

Complete the crossword
LOVe

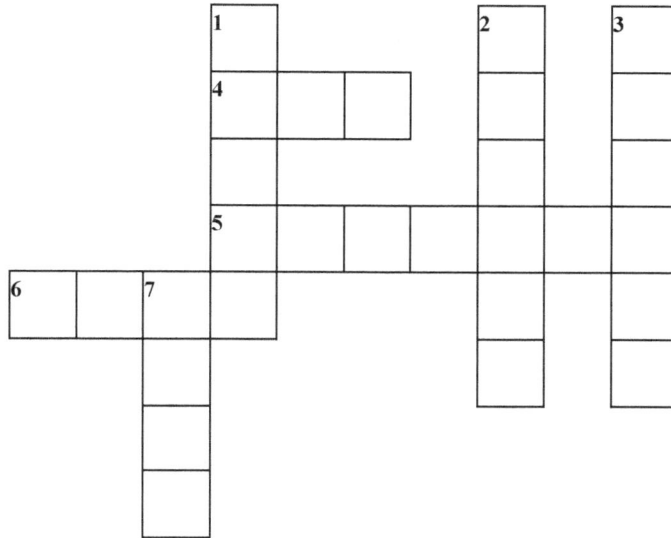

Across

4. To wrap your arms around someone

5. To treat or deal with others in a proper way

6. Something you say to make someone laugh

Down

1. Cleaning your room

2. Someone you do fun things with

3. To pay attention to what someone is saying

7. A peck on the cheek

WORD BANK

Chore
Friend
Hug
Joke
Kiss
Listen
Respect

Don't let negative words get to you,
they will only affect you if you let them!

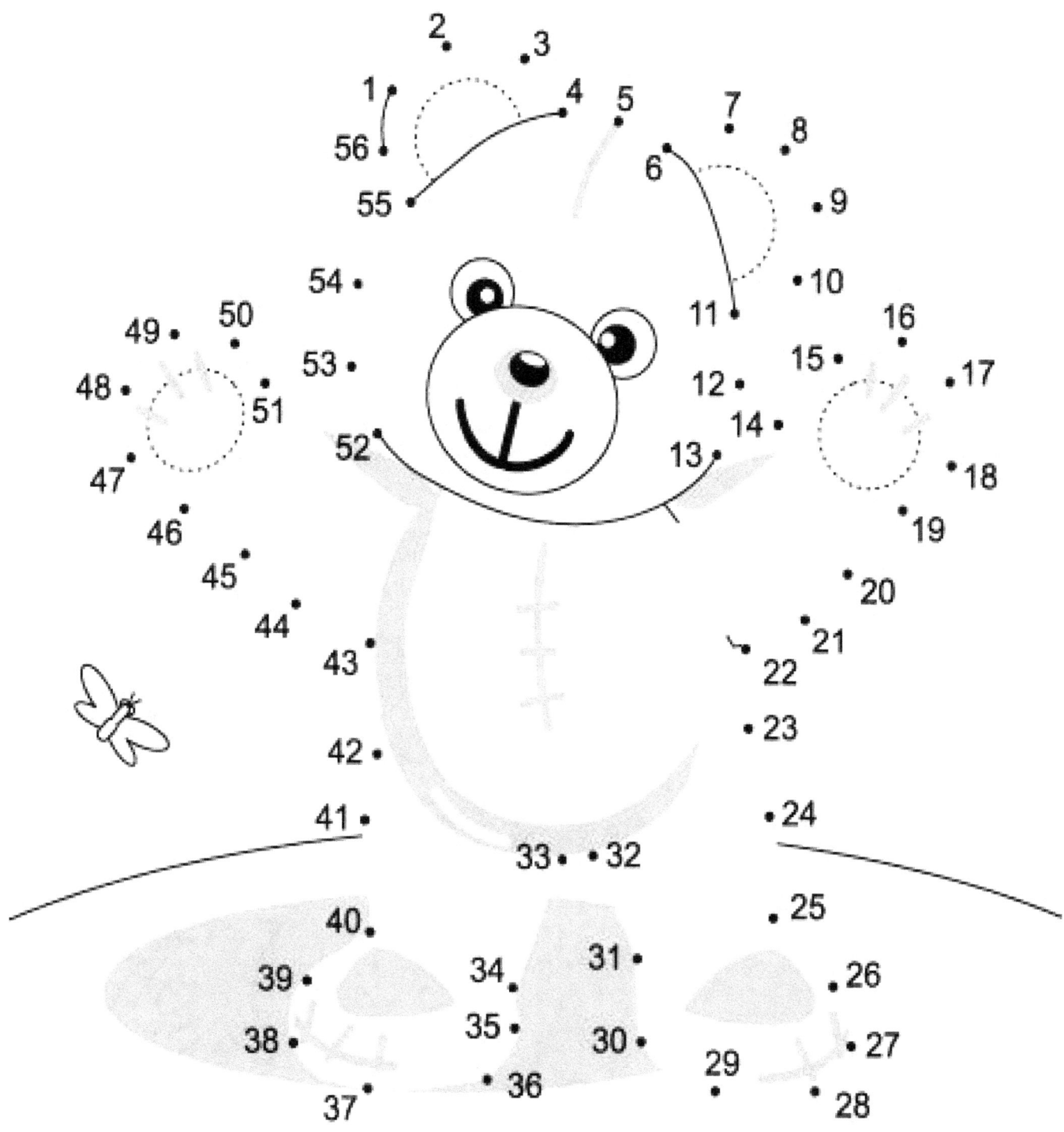

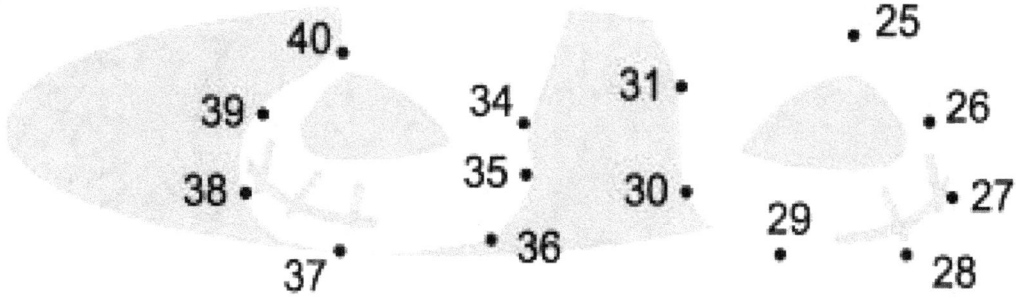

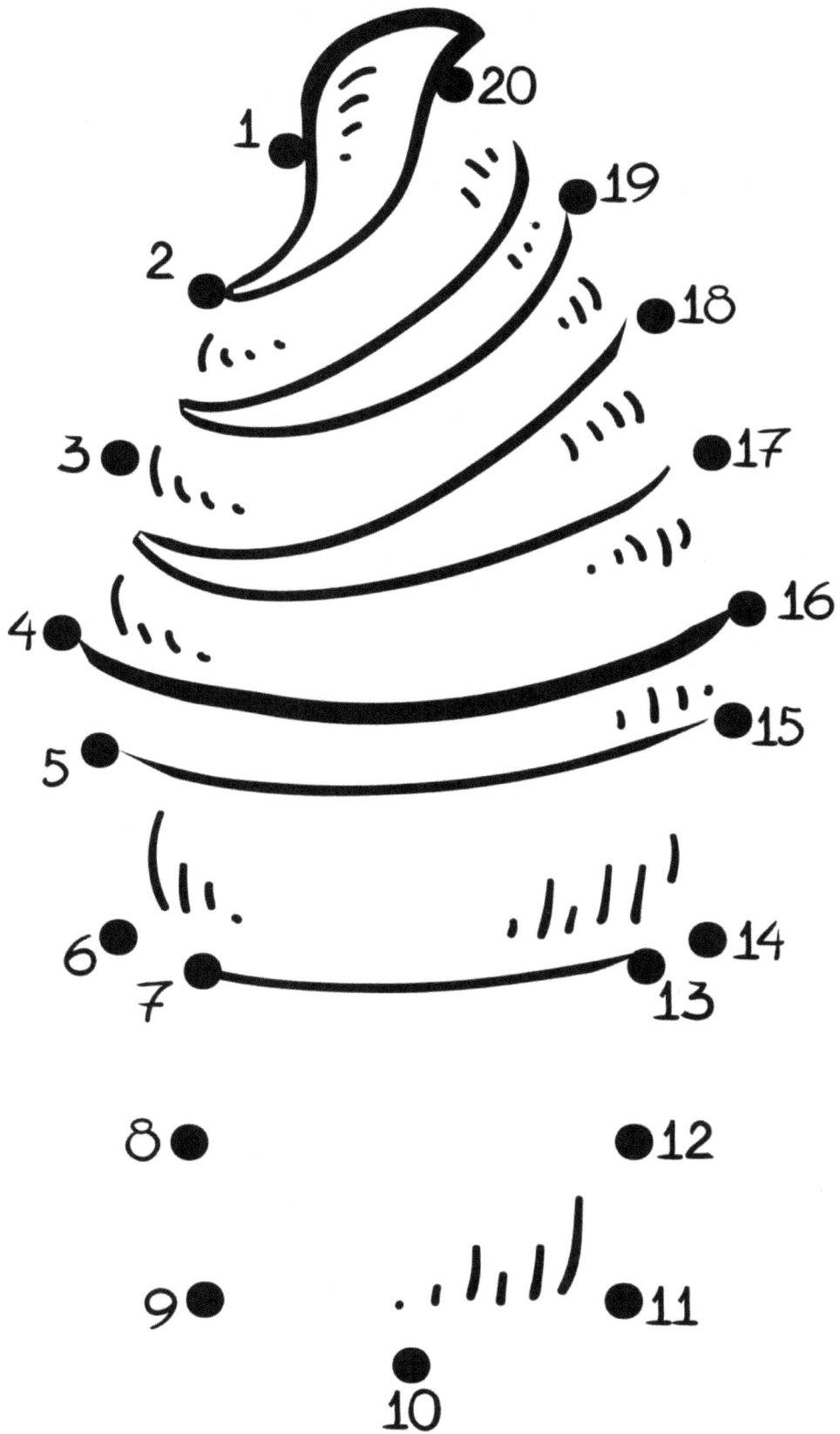

Find the words

Love-
Caring for something or someone very much

```
P E W H V F K K T T Z D
I E K V W O C O L W L G
H O C I D B Q P R T F H
S N S T L K G N O S C N
D C H E R I S H S A N G
N L E T A I C E R P P A
E O E R M L N I T V L D
I V Y R W D N E R O D A
R A G W N G M G C I F V
F B H O L F Y R H U C W
A L F C B P A L G V N R
H E M J A C B Y T V B L
```

ADORE
APPRECIATE
CARING
CHERISH

FONDNESS
FRIENDSHIP
LIKE
LOVABLE

Complete the picture, then color.

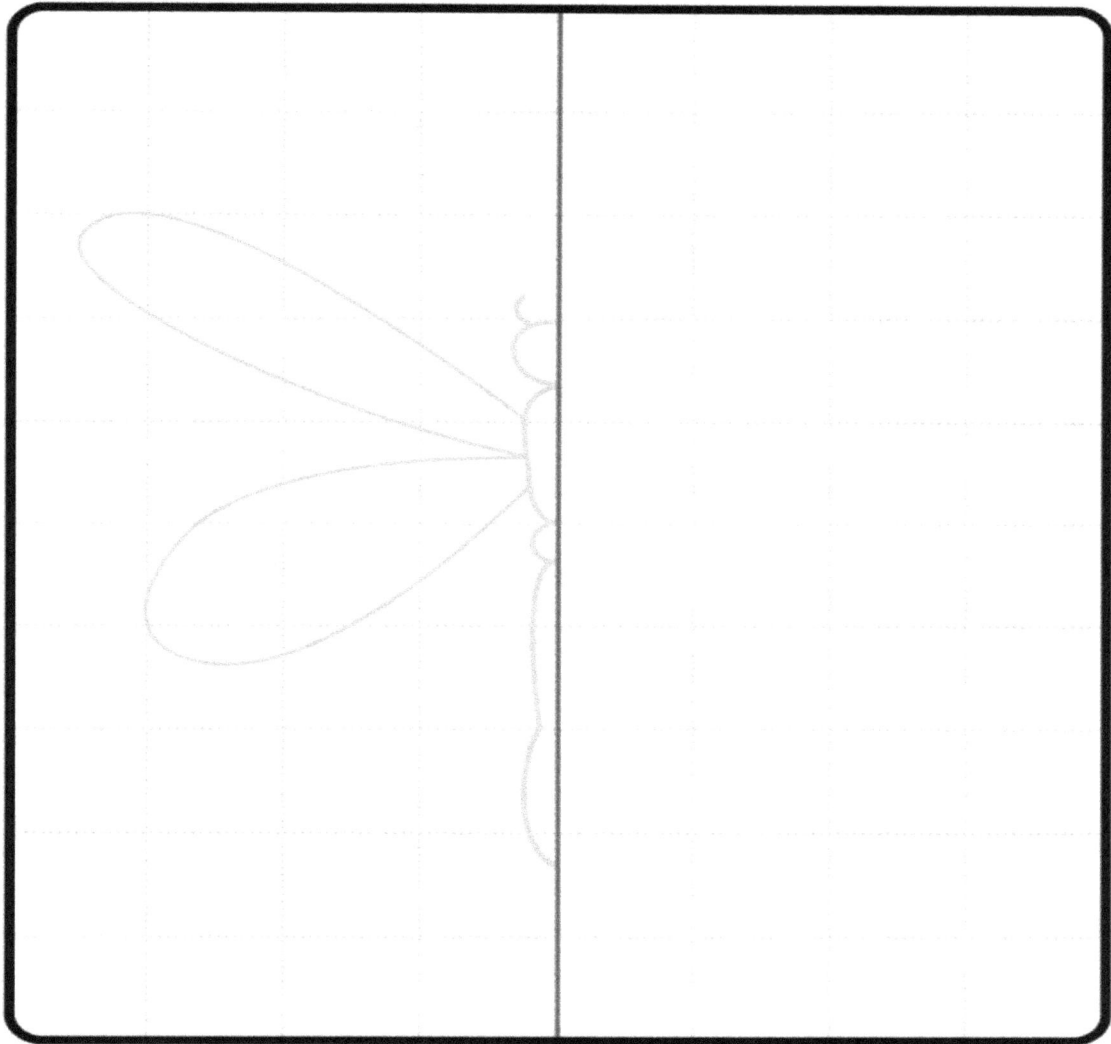

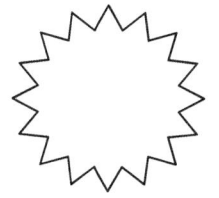

There is no fear

In my

Atmosphere!

Find the words

Smart-

Very good at learning or thinking about things

```
T K U V G L Z M R F T H
D N J W N F I Z P V D O
T N A G I L L E T N I T
W H D I C L E V E R H Q
R Y N I L D M V M G P U
O N G O U L M T I R Q I
R I F E I X I R P Q Z C
K A W T N S B R A L P K
D R G U M I E Q B F A U
Z B L A J Q U S Y B K H
X N R N E E K S I D D W
T T H B W K R F Y W G M
```

BRAINY

BRIGHT

BRILLIANT

CLEVER

GENIUS

INTELLIGANT

KEEN

QUICK

SMART

WISE

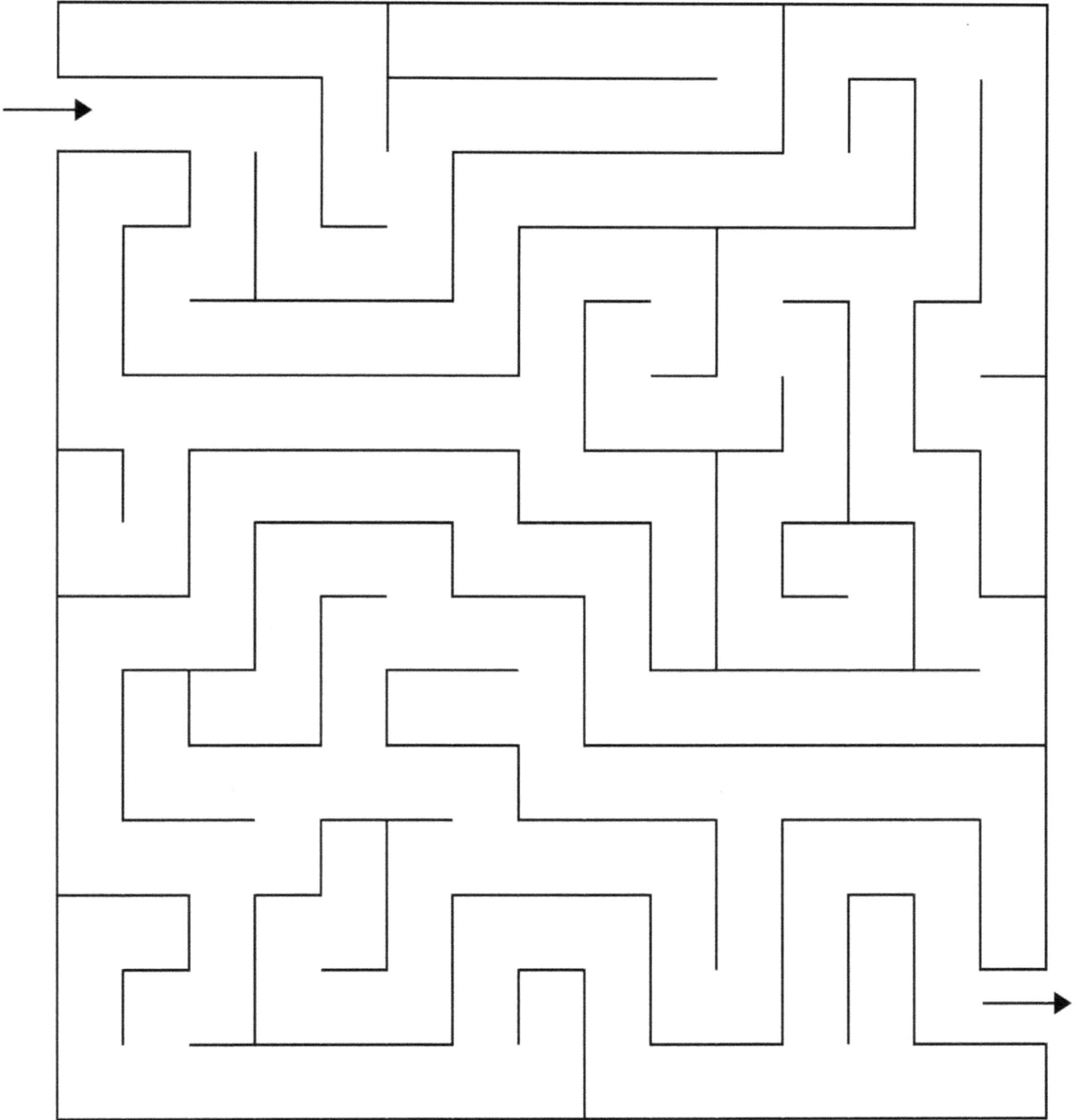

Match the letters with each number to decode an important message!

2	91	91

19	81	7	35	37	17

2	25	93

13	64	17	17	7	72	91	93

2	72	11	4
A	B	C	D

93	54	37	81
E	F	G	H

7	33	44	91
I	J	K	L

9	35	64	13
M	N	0	P

53	25	17	19
Q	R	S	T

28	51	6	5
U	V	W	X

26	0
Y	Z

Match the color with the number to complete the picture!

1 – White	5 - Pink
2 – Blue	6 - Orange
3 – Gray	7 - Brown
4 – Black	8 - Green

If you have enjoyed this activity book, check out our book for boys –

Confident Boys! Purpose & Confidence Building Activities for Boys

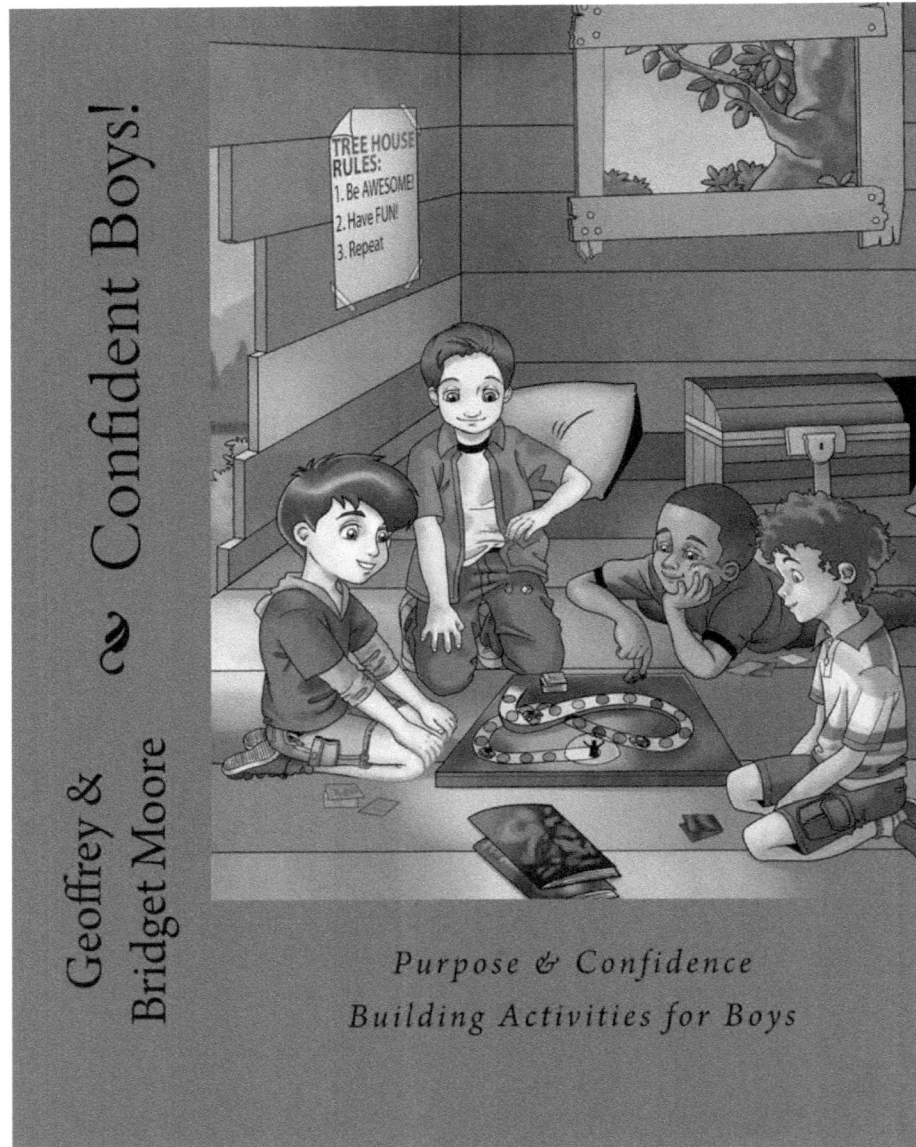

Geoffrey & Bridget Moore

Confident Boys!

Purpose & Confidence Building Activities for Boys

Available on Amazon.com

About the Author

Bridget is a Purpose Discovery Specialist who is eager to help children. She has been a volunteer teacher with her church for ten years- kids are her passion. She has a desire to help young girls find their purpose. Confident Girls! was written to help girls discover their gifts, build self-esteem and share it with the world!